SAIL LIKE A VIKING!

by Morris Ayin
illustrated by Richard Walz

Orlando   Boston   Dallas   Chicago   San Diego

Visit *The Learning Site!*
www.harcourtschool.com

Do you know about Vikings? Vikings
lived 1,000 years ago in Denmark,
Norway, and Sweden.

They lived by the sea far in the north
where it is very cold in the winter.

The Vikings were powerful people. They conquered many parts of the world. They captured land in England, France, Spain, and Italy. They also went to Russia, Iceland, Greenland—even North America.

How did they reach these far-away places?

The Vikings knew how to build strong
ships. They launched many ships. Their
fleet did not just crawl along. It sailed and
drifted fast on the open seas.

How did the Vikings build such good ships? Today, we don't have to wonder. Some of their old ships have been found in the earth.

In the 1960s, five Viking ships were found buried in Denmark. Later, nine more ships were found there. They were 1,000 years old!

Scientists studied the ships and the way they were built. This teaches us much about the Viking way of life.

People realized something else, too. Viking ships could be reproduced so that people would see what a Viking voyage was like.

In Denmark, some friends decided to imitate the Vikings of long ago. They built and launched a new Viking ship.

How did these new Vikings do it? Come on board and see.

To start, they chopped down tall oak trees. They cut and shaped the raw wood into boards, or planks. The planks were nearly 100 feet long!

Each plank had to be as thin as a finger! That way, the ship would be light and steady on the water.

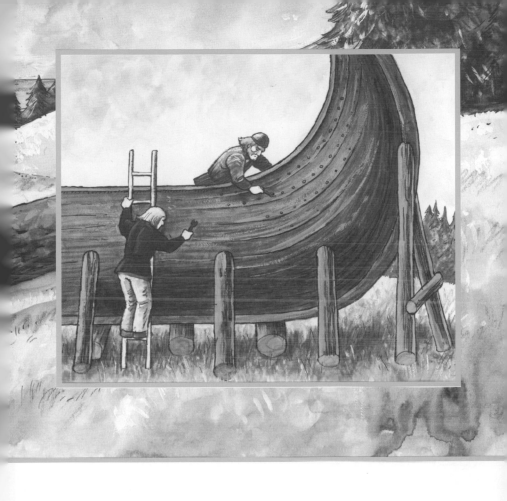

Then the wood planks were bolted together. The bolts the Vikings used were made of strong iron so the ship would not fall apart in the rough seas.

The Viking ship was better than any other ship in its time. That's because the Vikings added a special part to it. They put a long, thin strip of wood on the bottom of the boat. It is called a keel and is still used on ships today.

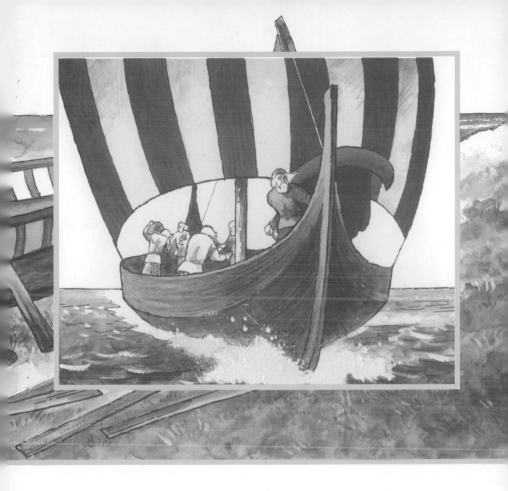

The keel made it easy to steer the ship, and it kept it steady in the water. The boat did not rock much, even if it was caught in rough water. Now, that's cozy!

Every Viking ship had a large, wool sail.
The Vikings made it with wool from
sheep. They wove the fibers together
tightly. Then they added tar and fat to
make the wool sail very strong.

When the reproduced Viking ship was finished and ready to go out to sea, each crew member had to row with an oar. A real Viking ship often had 20 or 30 pairs of oars.

On the ocean, the ship drifted with the wind. The crew didn't have to worry about a looming storm. The wool sail was strong, even when it became wet!

The Vikings used the sun and stars to guide them at sea. They also used birds to find land. Birds are good at finding land. Vikings often followed the birds!

Just like long ago, the people of Denmark, Sweden, and Norway live near the sea. Now that the Viking ships have been reproduced, people have learned a lot about the Vikings.

And people all over the world understand how the Vikings were able to travel to many distant lands.